THE ANIMAL KINGDOM

Amphibians

Bev Harvey

CHELSEA CLUBHOUSE

An Imprint of Chelsea House Publishers
A Haights Cross Communications ✈ Company
Philadelphia

Chelsea Clubhouse
1974 Sproul Road, Suite 400
Broomall, PA 19008-0914

The Chelsea House world wide web address is www.chelseahouse.com

Library of Congress Cataloging-in-Publication Data

Harvey, Bev.
  Amphibians / by Bev Harvey.
  p. cm. — (The animal kingdom)
  Summary: Introduces the physical characteristics and habits of various types of amphibians including frogs, toads, turtles, and salamanders.
  ISBN 0-7910-6983-4
  1. Amphibians—Juvenile literature. [1. Amphibians.] I. Title.
  QL644.2 .H38 2003
  597.8—dc21

                                                                    2002000920

First published in 2002 by
MACMILLAN EDUCATION AUSTRALIA PTY LTD
627 Chapel Street, South Yarra, Australia, 3141

Copyright © Bev Harvey 2002
Copyright in photographs © individual photographers as credited

Edited by Angelique Campbell-Muir
Page layout by Domenic Lauricella

Printed in China

Acknowledgements

Cover photograph: Blue poison dart (arrow) frog, courtesy of Rod Williams/Auscape.

ANT Photo Library, pp. 6 (bottom), 7 (bottom), 14 (eggs), 20, 22; Kathie Atkinson/Auscape, pp. 12, 14 (young frog with small tail), 15 (all); Erwin & Peggy Bauer/Auscape, p. 7 (top); John Brown—Oxford Scientific Films/Auscape, p. 9; Irvine Cushing—Oxford Scientific Films/Auscape, p. 5; Jean-Paul Ferrero/Auscape, pp. 8, 10; C. Andrew Henley/Auscape, pp. 7 (center), 16; Joe McDonald/Auscape, p. 4; John Shaw/Auscape, p. 13; Rod Williams/Auscape, pp. 1, 6 (top); Australian Picture Library/Corbis, pp. 11, 24; Jason Edwards/ Bio Images, pp. 17, 18, 21, 26; Coo-ee Picture Library, pp. 6 (center); Digital Stock, p. 23; Hans & Judy Beste/Lochman Transparencies, p. 14 (adult frog); Jiri Lochman/Lochman Transparencies, p. 19; U.S. Fish and Wildlife Service, pp. 28, 29; Henk.Wallays@skynet.be, pp. 25, 27.

While every care has been taken to trace and acknowledge copyright the publisher tenders their apologies for any accidental infringement where copyright has proved untraceable.

Contents

Amphibians

Amphibians are vertebrates. A vertebrate is an animal that has a backbone. Amphibians are **cold-blooded**. They do not have scales, and their skin is always moist.

Salamanders have moist skin.

Most frogs need to spend some time living in the water.

Nearly all amphibians begin their life in the water. As they grow, most amphibians go through a stage called **metamorphosis**. When they are adults, most amphibians can live on land. But many still need to live near water or in moist places. They will die if their skin dries out.

Types of Amphibians

There are many types of amphibians.

Frogs live all over the world except in extremely cold places and very dry deserts.

Toads also live in most areas of the world. Toads look like frogs, but they have bumps on their skin.

Salamanders live on every continent except Australia and Antarctica.

Newts are small salamanders that live in North America, Europe, and Asia.

Axolotls are salamanders that live in Mexico. They spend their whole lives in water.

Caecilians live in tropical regions of Central America, South America, and Asia.

Frogs and Toads

Frogs and toads live everywhere except the coldest and the driest places in the world. Frogs usually have smooth, moist skin. Most frogs live in or near water to keep their skin damp. Toads usually have dry, warty skin. Most adult toads only need to return to the water to have young.

This common toad has dry, warty skin.

This tree frog has a vocal sac.

Frogs and toads jump to move. Frogs have stronger back legs than toads. A frog can jump many times the length of its body.

Most male frogs and toads croak to attract their mates. Some frogs have **vocal sacs**, which puff out from their throats. Frogs with vocal sacs can make their calls louder.

Salamanders

A salamander has a tail and four legs. It looks similar to a lizard. But unlike a lizard, it has smooth skin rather than scales.

Salamanders are born in water or moist areas. Some adult salamanders live in or near water. Others can live on land. Many live in cool, dark, damp places. Newts live mostly on land. If a newt loses a leg, it can grow another one.

Caecilians

Most caecilians live underground, but some live in water. Those that live in water come to the surface to breathe air.

Eating Habits

Nearly all adult amphibians are carnivores. They eat meat such as worms, slugs, and insects. Frogs, toads, and some salamanders use their tongues to catch food. Caecilians use their teeth. Young amphibians, such as tadpoles, are herbivores. They eat tiny plants in the water.

Animals such as birds, snakes, and large
spiders eat amphibians. Some frogs and
toads have poisonous skin that can hurt or
kill the animals that eat them. Salamanders
use their tails for defense.

Young Amphibians

Some amphibians lay their eggs on land, but most lay their eggs in water. A female frog lays thousands of eggs at one time. The male frog **fertilizes** them. After a few days, tadpoles hatch. Tadpoles breathe through **gills** and swim by using their tails.

Adult frog

Eggs

Young frog
with small tail

A tadpole grows back legs first, then front legs. Finally, it grows lungs so it can breathe air. The young frog can now leave the pond.

Changing from a tadpole to a frog is called metamorphosis. Most amphibians go through metamorphosis. Some amphibians take only about a week to develop into adults, but others take months or sometimes years.

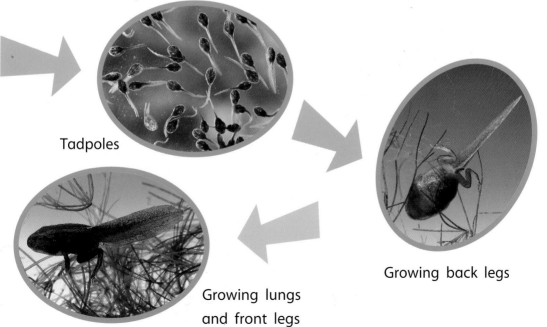

Tadpoles

Growing back legs

Growing lungs and front legs

Pet Salamanders

Some people keep salamanders as pets. Pet salamanders live in aquariums. Owners need to know how to care for their salamanders.

Some salamanders need to live in moist sand or dirt. Other salamanders need to have water and land. Salamanders such as axolotls live only in water. Axolotls breathe through gills on their necks.

Pet salamanders must be kept moist. If they dry out, they will die. Salamanders should not be held because traces of salt on human hands hurt their skin. Salamanders are nocturnal. This means they are more active at night. Aquariums do not need extra lighting.

Pet salamanders need to be fed at least three times a week. Most salamanders eat crickets and other insects, worms, and small spiders. Pet salamanders need to eat a variety of food to give them a balanced diet.

Many salamanders lay their eggs in water. The young live in water and breathe through gills. They go through metamorphosis to change into adults. It is important not to keep large salamanders with smaller ones. Larger salamanders sometimes eat smaller ones.

Tree Frogs

Tree frogs live in areas with mild to tropical temperatures. Tree frogs have flat, sticky pads on their toes. These pads help tree frogs climb trees. Tree frogs can also climb on buildings and into mailboxes.

Tree frogs vary in size. Some are only as long as a person's fingernail. The Australian green tree frog is about 4 inches (10 centimeters) long. It is found in northern Australia and on nearby islands.

21

Tree frogs mainly eat insects and spiders. Some may eat small animals such as snakes. Most tree frogs are nocturnal and hunt at night.

Red-eyed tree frogs live in tropical rain forests. Females lay their eggs under leaves that hang over water. When the tadpoles hatch, they fall into the water. The tadpoles turn into frogs in about 11 weeks.

Caecilians are the only amphibians without legs. They range in size from about 4 inches (10 centimeters) to about 20 inches (51 centimeters). Caecilians live underground or in water.

Caecilians have jaws, teeth, and a bony skeleton. A caecilian's eyes are usually covered by skin, so it uses tentacles to sense its surroundings. Caecilians can be many colors including yellow, purple, orange, and gray.

Caecilians eat insects, **larvae**, earthworms, and termites. They find their food in the tropical swamps where they live.

Caecilians have their young in one of three ways. Some caecilians lay eggs. Some give birth to live young. And with some caecilians, the eggs hatch inside the female. The young live inside her body until full grown.

Endangered Houston Toads

The Houston toad lives in Texas. It lives on land but needs water to breed. It also needs loose sand to burrow in during dry summers or cold winters. The Houston toad has lost much of its **habitat** because land has been cleared for farms and houses. It has become **endangered**.

Glossary

cold-blooded   an animal whose body temperature changes to match the temperature of the air, ground, or water around it

endangered   a type of animal or plant that may soon die out

fertilize   to join male and female cells in order to produce young

gill   part of an animal's body that allows it to take in oxygen from water

habitat   the natural area where an animal or plant normally lives or grows

hibernating   being still, as if sleeping, during winter

larva   a growth stage some animals go through after hatching from their eggs and before becoming adults; larvae look very different from adults; tadpoles are the larva stage of frogs; insect larvae look similar to worms.

metamorphosis   the change in the form of an animal as it grows to adulthood

vocal sac   a pouch made of skin that fills with air; vocal sacs make frogs' calls louder.

Index